Olana Landscapes

Olana Landscapes

The World of Frederic E. Church

Gerald L. Carr

Foreword by James A. Ryan

RIZZOLI
NEW YORK

First published in the United States of America in 1989 by
RIZZOLI INTERNATIONAL PUBLICATIONS, INC.
300 Park Avenue South, New York, NY 10010

Copyright © 1989 Gerald L. Carr.

Library of Congress Catalog Card Number 87-61932
ISBN 0-8478-1146-8

Designed by Stephen Kruse
Printed in Singapore

This book has been produced with the generous support
of a grant from the Graham Foundation for Advanced
Studies in the Fine Arts.

To my parents

Contents

Acknowledgements

Many organizations and individuals helped make this publication possible. Deserving of special appreciation are the staff of Olana State Historic Site itself, in particular the Site Manager, James A. Ryan, who always gives unstintingly of his time to those interested in the property over which he ably presides, and who was kind enough to write a foreword to the book. Other staff members who bore with grace my propensity to look at the skies above Olana and answered my questions with diligence were Jane Churchill, Robin Eckerle, Yvonne Smith, Clayton Andrus, Peter De Luca, David Fagan, Leonard Miller, Anthony Novak, Paul Podmijersky, Bruce Puckett, David Spier, Joe Stewart, Kevin Walsh, and Robert Williams. Ellen McClelland Lesser, whose expertise in Victorian floral design is well known to visitors at Olana, cordially allowed me to consult the results of her comprehensive research on the park and gardens of the estate. Betsy Fahlman of Arizona State University supplied a crucial morsel of documentation about the building of Olana, and Barry Hopkins furnished detailed information about the topography of the Catskills.

I must add a full measure of gratitude to the Friends of Olana for permitting many diversions of my energies toward this endeavor while maintaining their sights — and my own — on a still larger project, a complete catalogue of the works of Frederic Edwin Church still housed at Olana. Professor David Huntington, who more than anyone was responsible for the preservation of Olana two decades ago, also introduced the property to me through the medium of photography at about that time. My wife Annemarie offered inspiration and judicious suggestions throughout the evolution of the project. My parents provided constant encouragement.

This book was supported by a grant from the Graham Foundation for Advanced Studies in the Fine Arts. Additional funding was provided by the Friends of Olana. The following people, all of whom are deeply knowledgeable in matters of American art, also generously contributed financial assistance: Alexander Acevedo, of Alexander Gallery, New York; Warren Adelson, of Coe Kerr Gallery, New York; Michael Altman, of Altman Burke Fine Art, New York; Stuart Feld, of Hirschl and Adler Galleries, New York; Neil Morris, New York; Mrs. John C. Newington and Florence Levins, of the Cropsey-Newington Foundation, Hasting-on-Hudson, New York; James Graham, of Graham Gallery, New York; Alfred C. Harrison, Jr., of North Point Gallery, San Francisco; James Maroney, of James Maroney, Inc., New York; Robert Vose, Jr., of Vose Galleries, Boston; and Gerold Wunderlich, of Gerold Wunderlich and Company, New York.

G.L.C.
April 1989

FOREWORD

erald Carr became aware of Frederic Church and of Olana, Church's estate at Hudson, New York, as a graduate student in art history at the University of Michigan under the tutelage of the distinguished Church scholar David C. Huntington. While working in England several years later, Dr. Carr unearthed valuable information about the London exhibitions of Church's major paintings, among them *Niagara Falls, The Heart of the Andes,* and the then unlocated *Icebergs.* He soon augmented his studies in England with the first of many research-oriented visits to Olana State Historic Site in the fall of 1978. When *The Icebergs* was dramatically rediscovered one year later at a remand home near Manchester, England, bought at auction in New York and presented to the Dallas Museum of Art, the museum invited Dr. Carr to write a monograph on their newly acquired treasure.

In 1983, at the request of the Friends of Olana, a private, non-profit service organization for the site, Dr. Carr returned to Olana to begin work on a catalogue of the more than nine hundred pencil and oil sketches and finished works of art by Church in the Olana collections. Dr. Carr's painstaking examination of extensive archives at Olana and elsewhere, and of myriad newspapers and other published materials from Church's lifetime, provided much new data on each work of art at Olana and permitted its significance within Church's oeuvre to be reassessed.

The perception of Olana as one of Church's major works of art owes much to David C. Huntington's *Landscapes of Frederic Edwin Church,* published in 1966. Here, too, Dr. Carr has followed in the footsteps of his mentor, uncovering new aspects of Olana's history and character. Augmented by the efforts of other scholars, this recent research has clarified and enriched our understanding of the estate, the aesthetic motivations of its creator, and its place in the broader context of the architecture and decorative art of its period. Though Olana survives virtually intact, a legacy from Church's hand and eye, cultural references have shifted so drastically since the artist's death in 1900 that visitors to the place described by Huntington as a "typification of an America that is no more" may be puzzled, possibly mistaking it for an idiosyncratic fantasy rather than as a carefully designed and executed work of art.

Olana is in fact a conscientious design that may be understood as comprising three parts: the house, the landscaped grounds that surround it, and the distant views that complete the concept. The tripartite composition was the focus of Church's attention. Records document that Church's methods in participating in the creation of Olana were far different from those he employed in the building and furnishing of Cozy Cottage, the first house he built on his Hudson estate, which had been completed in 1861, just ten years earlier. His hundreds of pencil and oil sketches for all aspects of the second, much more ambitious building, his careful use of color in all its gradations to denote the functions of individual rooms and to interrelate them, the two-dimensional stencils he designed for their embellishment, and even his careful selecting and placing of the furnishings speak to Church's paramount purpose: to suffuse himself and his family in an atmosphere of "sweetness and light" (in the nineteenth-century parlance).

Believing the landscape painter to be the premier landscape gardener, Church began in 1860 to lay out roads, to plant thousands of trees, and, at a later date, to dredge a pond on his two-hundred-and-fifty-acre property. The landscaping of the grounds not only acts as the foreground of an extensive view but also constitutes a kind of multi-dimensional landscape painting. The design is premised on aesthetic principles of the Sublime, Beautiful and Picturesque prevalent in landscape gardening in Church's youth, when land, trees and water were "sweetly mingled" (the words of architect and garden designer A.J. Downing) in a harmonious whole. Though the Olana landscape appears to be naturally formed and almost untouched by man, it is in actuality as artificial, as carefully wrought, as the house that is its central feature.

The grand panoramic views of the Hudson River and the Catskill Mountains beyond may therefore be described as Church's own handiwork, as well.

In 1846, shortly after concluding his two-year studentship with Thomas Cole in Catskill, Church wrote to his teacher, "The recollection of the blue mountains [the Catskills] is as fresh and vivid to me as the day I last saw them." As a mature artist, Church depicted that landscape so often that as one looks out at the view of the "blue mountains" from his house, his paintings inevitably come to mind. To note the diverse antecedents that were invoked in the fashioning of Olana is useful, but it must be remembered that the controlling factor of the singular design was Church's unique genius. Dr. Carr's knowledgeable text and superb photographs serve as a cogent illustration of the continued power of Church's inspired vision.

Olana, widely regarded as a work of art in the nineteenth century, has been forgotten for much of the twentieth. Happily, for the past twenty years, recognition of this extraordinary place has been reviving as surely as has the popularity of Church's paintings. The estate remained in the Church family until 1966, when, through the efforts of Olana Preservation, a short-lived organization founded to purchase and preserve the estate, it was rescued from dispersal by the State of New York. Under the administration of the Office of Parks, Recreation and Historic Preservation, Taconic Region, the grounds and house are being restored to their appearance of 1891, the year that Church considered his work on them to be at an end.

Olana was saved so that visitors could continue to experience the pleasure the artist intended for his family and guests. The State of New York invites the public to walk on the old carriage drives, to watch the sun set behind the mountains, and to tour the home. It is my hope that each reader of Dr. Carr's book will be drawn to Olana to enjoy its bounteous charms in person.

James A. Ryan
Site Manager
Olana State Historic Site
Hudson, New York

INTRODUCTION

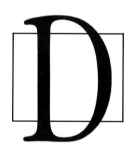uring the summer of 1880, the American landscape painter Frederic Edwin Church (1826–1900) and his wife Isabel Carnes Church (1836–99) began referring to their country house, recently erected on a hilltop overlooking the Hudson River three miles south of the city of Hudson, New York, as "Olana." Since then, the appellation has remained firmly attached to the Persian-style edifice and the two-hundred-and-fifty-acre property surrounding it.

Today, more than twenty years after it was designated a Historic Site of the State of New York, Olana is nationally renowned as a comprehensive museum of Church's art; a major specimen of American Victorian taste in architecture, decoration, and garden design; and a splendid scenic environment stretching along the horizon as far as the eye can see. Tens of thousands of visitors annually take advantage of this unique opportunity to enter Church's world and to enjoy the beauty of the estate and its surroundings. The architecture of the house combines Persian, Indian, Chinese, Mexican, Italian, French Renaissance, Gothic and an undercurrent of Romanesque flavors. These antecedents transport the visitor around the world and across centuries of human history at the same time that they signal the eclectic sensibilities of the painter and his wife, and of the late nineteenth century in general. The Moorish element predominates in the bouquet of stylistic and cultural references. To be charmed by Olana today is to sympathize with those of Church's contemporaries whose creativity responded to the romance of the Near East: Verdi's *Aida* (1871) and Rimsky-Korsakov's *Scheherazade* (1888) precisely bracket its construction phases. Nevertheless, the Hudson River Valley setting in which Church placed his home speaks more to the here and now. While it, too, conjures potent historical associations, those extending back through European colonists and indigenous Indian tribes, it is immediately intelligible to anyone who appreciates the out-of-doors. From both afar and nearby, the house attracts the eye, and the view from the top of the hill is the finest commanded by a domestic building in the northeastern United States.

Isabel Carnes Church, ca. 1865, and Frederic Edwin Church, ca. 1866.
New York State
Office of Parks, Recreation and Historic Preservation
Olana State Historic Site

The allure and accessibility of Olana in our day should not obscure the fact that originally it was a private residence. From its isolated position five hundred feet above the Hudson River and three miles from the nearest large settlement, the Churches could rear their children, entertain guests and conduct their lives as they wished. Yet they also conceived the building and its environment to be a kind of monument and a statement of complex, comprehensive significance. The name Olana is the key that unlocks the symbolic meaning of their home. Only one known document from the couple's lifetimes refers to the title selection process. In September 1890, as Mr. Church was completing an addition to the house (a studio connected to the main structure by a porticoed gallery), a visiting reporter for the *Boston Herald* newspaper wrote that Mrs. Church had chosen the designation because it was "an old Latin name for a place in Persia, to which the artist's home bears resemblance in situation." The reporter's statement is essentially correct. According to the Greco-Roman geographer Strabo (ca. 63 B.C. – ca. 21 A.D.), *Olane* was a fortress and "treasure-storehouse" not far from Artaxata, the ancient Persian capital on the Araxes

(Aras) River which empties into the Caspian Sea. A few eighteenth and nineteenth century authors identified Strabo's *Olane* with *Alanjek,* a hilltop stronghold mentioned in the chronicles of the Mongol conqueror Tamerlane and located above a tributary of the Araxes in present-day Soviet Armenia, just north of the Russian-Iranian border. Church owned an English translation of Strabo's *Geography,* given to him by his wife on Christmas 1879, and *A Second Journey through Persia, Armenia and Asia Minor* by James Morier, published in 1818, in which Strabo's *Olana* (now spelled with two a's) is equated with *Alanjek* and is pinpointed on a foldout map.

In the Churches' day, as in ours, that region of the Near East was inflamed by territorial disagreements, but it was also associated with the biblical origins, destruction and regeneration of mankind in the remote past. These older associations, as well as those with Persia in general, were paramount for the Churches. Situated some sixty miles southeast of Mount Ararat, the presumed landing place of Noah's Ark, in an area popularly believed to have been the site of the earthly Paradise, the first Olana had overlooked a fertile river valley. The new Olana was much the same — an exotic Near Eastern palace and repository, adapted as domicile for the most famous of the second-generation Hudson River School painters and his family, a focal point within an Edenic landscape garden, and an observatory from which to survey some of the finest scenery in North America.

The only large painting by his own hand that Church introduced into the early interior decor at Olana underscores the first part of this interpretation. *El Khasné, Petra,* completed in 1874, and presented by the artist to his wife and installed in the Sitting Room of Olana a year later, celebrates his most adventurous and enthralling experience in the Near East, a three-week expedition to the dead city of Petra (in present-day Jordan) in February and March 1868. The name *El Khasné,* bestowed on the foremost rock-cut tomb (2nd cen. A.D.) at Petra by Arab tribesmen who erroneously believed that the building had been fabricated for an Egyptian Pharaoh, means "The Treasury." For Church, *El Khasné* became a synonym for *Olana.*

EL KHASNE, PETRA, 1874
Oil on canvas, 60½ × 50¼″
New York State
Office of Parks, Recreation and Historic Preservation
Olana State Historic Site

Church understandably was proud of Olana, because it was his creation. Partly in jest, partly in earnest, he wrote in July 1869 to a close friend and colleague, the Albany, New York, sculptor Erastus Dow Palmer (1817–1904): "About an hour this side of Albany is the center of the world — I own it." He penned the remark less than two weeks after he and his family had returned from a twenty-month tour of Europe and the Near East, and about a year before he began work on the house. The timing hints at his jubilation as the conception was taking shape in his mind, and the remark itself foretells the name for the estate eventually chosen by Mrs. Church: Armenians had long believed that Mount Ararat was "the center of the earth." Palmer knew that the painter already had begun to develop the property extensively after acquiring the initial portions of it in 1860, and that he planned to become absorbed in its full realization. The concentrated efforts Church had lavished on his major paintings during the 1850s and 1860s gradually were redirected to Olana.

In 1860 Church had commissioned Richard Morris Hunt (1827–95), whose career as one of America's fashionable architects was then getting underway, to design a cottage better suited to his family's needs than an existing farmhouse on the property. Over the following four decades, Church supervised a functioning farm, erected service buildings, altered and demolished other structures, installed cultivated gardens, and organized the entire estate as a landscape garden in the Picturesque style. For the house itself, he served as chief architect for the first phase of its construction in 1870–72 and as sole architect for its extension in 1888–91. Throughout the long process, he delved into every detail of the design, drafting the bulk of preparatory and working drawings, superintending workmen, purchasing tons of building materials and having most of the stone quarried on the estate. Along with his wife, he also was responsible for the acquisition, arrangement and sometimes the design and manufacture of the artistic interior decor.

During nearly forty years in the nineteenth century, Church had fashioned the land and structures Olana comprises into his most elaborate work of art, an enduring aesthetic synthesis of artifact and nature dedicated first of all to his family. Throughout the process of its fabrication, his commitment was undiminished. He told the *Boston Herald* reporter in 1890 that as long as he remained its occupant, Olana would never be completed. As the journalist explained, "every year he conceives some plan by which he can add to its attractiveness and convenience." In so saying, Church acknowledged that his home, like the landscape of which it is a part, the human sensitivity that produced it, and the family that inspired it, was ever-changing.

The earliest and largest parcel of the Olana estate was called Wynson Breezy Farm, after Winsum Brisee, a late eighteenth-century owner. It was situated at the foot of *Sienghenbergh* (a Dutch word meaning "Long Hill"), atop which the main house now stands. Church concluded the purchase in March 1860 and hired the previous proprietor to stay on to manage it. The date is noteworthy for two reasons. At that time, Church stood at the peak of his career. In a period when landscape painting had evolved into the national art form, two of his recent epic canvases, *Niagara Falls* and *The Heart of the Andes,* had captured the imaginations of tens of thousands of viewers on both sides of the Atlantic and had lifted him to the rank of "America's greatest artist" (the words of a compatriot). His claim to that title was soon substantiated by a somewhat smaller masterwork, *Twilight in the Wilderness* (1860; Cleveland Museum of Art), then underway in his New York studio, and *The Icebergs,* a monumental painting developed from sketches made during a journey to the Labrador coast in mid-1859. In addition, Church was preparing to be married. Besides fulfilling the promise many observers had discerned in his early works such as *New England Scenery* (1851; George Walter Vincent Smith Museum, Springfield, Ma.), the masterpieces of 1857–61 had focused unprecedented attention on his private life. The peripatetic, genial, professionally ambitious yet socially reserved artist found himself in demand as a cultural spokesman, a celebrity and a most eligible bachelor. His acquisition of the "farm" (as he referred to his landholding for several years after his marriage in June 1860) therefore marked a turning point in his life. The rural dwelling served as the couple's primary residence, while its setting signified Church's new professional and marital status, and represented a release from the bustling New York art world.

Two writers who spoke with the painter late in his life report that he studied the views and contours of the Hudson River Valley for three years before deciding on where to settle. Yet in historical retrospect, his decision seems virtually inevitable. An explanation of his site selection offered in August 1884 by a family friend is close to the mark. As the friend told the Reverend Francis Nicholl Zabriskie (1830–91), "While a pupil of Thomas Cole at Catskill, Mr. Church was in the habit of roaming over the adjacent country on both sides of the river, in search of the picturesque. His favorite spot was a lofty hill about three miles south of Hudson, just south of the beautiful Mount Merino. And when in later years he thought of building a home, he realized an early dream of rearing it on this commanding eminence." A drawing preserved at Olana confirms that in May 1845, at the midpoint of his two-year period of study with Cole (1801–48), the premier first-generation painter of the Hudson River School, the youthful pupil and his master had stood together on Red Hill, where Cole already had sketched on several occasions during the 1830s. Most of Red Hill was included in Church's purchase of 1860, and the remainder was annexed to the Olana estate in 1877 (see map, page 8). Hence, when the mature Church returned to the region to obtain property for himself and his bride-to-be, he gravitated naturally to the locale his mentor had introduced him to fifteen years earlier. Church owed to Cole a lifelong affection for the Catskills and an acquaintance with the site of his future residence. At Olana, Church chose to live among scenes he associated with his artistic awakening.

Although there are important differences between the paintings of teacher and pupil, it would be fair to say that most aspects of Church's pictorial art evolved from Cole's work. Church would have welcomed the comparison. He held his master's work in high esteem and collected examples of it: two paintings by Cole are still at Olana, and several other examples of Cole's art passed through Church's hands from the late 1850s onward. He also maintained

NIAGARA FALLS, 1857
Oil on canvas, 42½ × 90½"
In the collection of The Corcoran Gallery of Art;
Museum Purchase, Gallery Fund, 1876

THE HEART OF THE ANDES, 1859
Oil on canvas, 66⅛ × 119¼″
The Metropolitan Museum of Art;
Bequest of Mrs. David Dows, 1909 (09.95)

6

THE ICEBERGS, 1861
Oil on canvas, 64½ × 112³⁄₈″
Dallas Museum of Fine Arts;
Anonymous Gift 1979.28

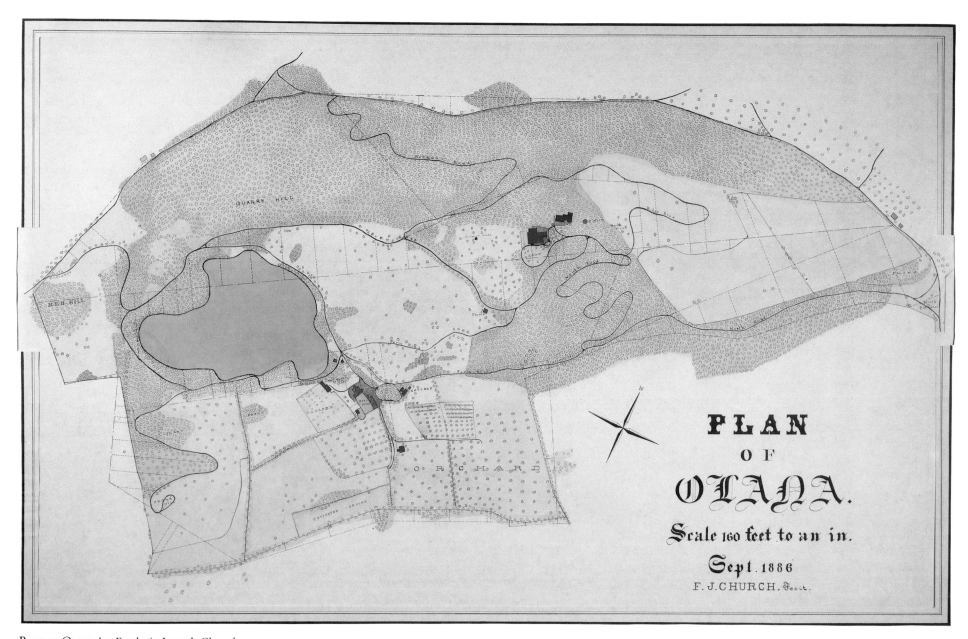

PLAN OF OLANA by Frederic Joseph Church
Ink, pencil and watercolor on paper, 22¹/₈ × 36¹/₄″
New York State
Office of Parks, Recreation and Historic Preservation
Olana State Historic Site

lifelong ties with Cole's family, and cherished the memory of the formative guidance Cole had given him and the scenery in which the learning had taken place. The connections to Cole extended even to Church's wedding. The officiating minister, the Reverend Louis Legrand Noble (1813–82), a talented man of letters who wrote eloquently on behalf of *The Heart of the Andes* and *The Icebergs* and traveled with Church to Labrador in 1859, was Cole's biographer and former pastor.

E ven as he took possession of Wynson Breezy Farm, Church must have had his eye on the summit of Sienghenbergh. Finally in late 1867, as he was preparing to leave for the Old World with his wife, year-old son and mother-in-law, he bought the remainder of the hill, paying almost three times the price per acre as he had for the original farm property.

T he journey abroad postponed and fundamentally altered Church's building plans. Most of his compatriot colleagues had taken European tours early in their professional lives, but he saved his until he was past forty; having already accomplished a great deal, he desired a change of direction in his career. His main objective was the Near East, by then an area of increasing worldwide commercial, theological, archaeological and artistic interest, yet still an unusual venue for an American painter. After stopping briefly in Alexandria, Egypt, he and his family traveled in present-day Lebanon, Jordan, Syria, Turkey and Greece. His experiences in those countries produced no less than an about-face in the subject matter and underlying meaning of his work. Whereas his pictures of New World themes before 1868 exuded (in the words of a perceptive contemporary) "the lavishness and splendor of youth. . .the ardor of that adventurous time [of life]. . .[and] Nature in her regal robes, in her hour of triumph, in her winged coquetry, and in the dreamy langours of her locked solitude," his later paintings of Mediterranean subjects were tinged with a contemplative, sadder poetry of the spirit appropriate to "this maturer phase of the genius of Church." The exultation and freshness of New World natural history were supplanted, at least in part, by subdued reminders of Old World history of mankind.

LANDSCAPE, HUDSON VALLEY, September 1870
Oil on paper, 13⅞ × 12⁹⁄₁₆ ″
Given by Louis P. Church;
Courtesy of the Cooper-Hewitt Museum,
Smithsonian Institution/Art Resource, New York, NY
1917-4-582c

SUNSET IN HUDSON VALLEY, ca. 1870
Oil on paper, 12 × 20″
Given by Louis P. Church;
Courtesy of the Cooper-Hewitt Museum,
Smithsonian Institution/Art Resource, New York, NY
1917-4-864

The Hudson Valley in Winter from Olana, ca. 1871–2
Oil on paperboard, 11¾ × 18¼ ″
New York State
Office of Parks, Recreation and Historic Preservation
Olana State Historic Site

NIGHTFALL AT OLANA, August 1872
Oil on paperboard, 9½ × 14⅛″
Given by Louis P. Church;
Courtesy of the Cooper-Hewitt Museum,
Smithsonian Institution/Art Resource, New York, NY
1917-4-587

That shift of emphasis in Church's paintings is mirrored to some extent in Olana, but a comparison between canvases and architecture must be made with care, since there is nothing about the house that could be called tired, melancholy, or for that matter topographically misplaced. The Churches' sojourn in the Old World had expanded and reshaped their tastes without reducing their love for the Hudson Valley or for their American heritage. On a scale that is at once domestically intimate and geographically grand, Olana enacts a meeting of East and West. Nor would it be just to Church himself if Olana were regarded primarily or even secondarily as the status symbol of an eminently successful artist. In the first place, though his earlier achievements such as *Niagara Falls* and *The Heart of the Andes* remained much admired, Church's reputation as a practicing painter was declining by the time the house was under construction. Another artist in that position might have been tempted to rest on his laurels or to lament his lessening glory, but Church maintained a decent level of studio productivity while devoting increased energy to his personal pursuits. The foremost of those pursuits was the building of Olana.

In the second place, his priorities had changed. Tragically, during a ten-day period in March 1865, his first two children were carried away by diphtheria. In the wake of those devastating events, the Churches rebuilt their family with the birth of a son in New York in 1866, another son in Rome in 1869, and a son and a daughter at Olana in 1870 and 1871, respectively. Olana therefore exemplified the energy and determination of a mature man and his wife who were fulfilling a favored dream, reestablishing and rearing a family, and commemorating recent shared adventures unlike any they would experience for the rest of their lives.

CLOUDS OVER OLANA, August, 1872
Oil on paperboard, 8¹¹/₁₆ × 12¹/₈″
New York State
Office of Parks, Recreation and Historic Preservation
Olana State Historic Site

I

THE HOUSE

Before departing the United States in 1867, Church asked Richard Morris Hunt to design a country seat suitable for the summit of Sienghenbergh. Upon his return, however, Church set aside Hunt's proposals in favor of a Persian-style design mostly of his own making. During his travels abroad, he had gathered ideas for all facets of his home-to-be. While passing through the Danube and the Rhone valleys, for example, he took particular note of castles and smaller edifices crowning rocky promontories. In the Near East, he was sufficiently impressed with sure-footed, docile Lebanese donkeys to import three specimens of the breed to Olana in 1869. He augmented his considerable firsthand knowledge of Near Eastern architecture and decoration through his purchases of sumptuously illustrated books published in Paris: Pascal Coste's *Monuments modernes de la Perse* (1867), Jules Bourgoin's *Les Arts Arabes* (1868) and E. Collinot's *Ornements de la Perse* (1882). A copy of each of those volumes is still at Olana.

For professional assistance and advice, Church turned to Calvert Vaux (1824–95), a prominent architect and brother-in-law of one of Church's former pupils, the landscape painter Jervis McEntee (1828–91). Vaux acted as consultant on essential utilitarian concerns such as structural stability, plumbing, and proper fit of all the parts. Evidently he also assisted in the evolution of the design, but there especially, Church's preferences held sway. The task was by turns exhilarating, frustrating and amusing. As Church wrote to his fellow painter John Ferguson Weir (1841–1926) in June 1871: ". . . having undertaken to get my architecture from Persia where I have never been nor any of my friends either — I am obliged to imagine Persian architecture — then embody it on paper and explain it to a lot of mechanics whose ideal of architecture is wrapped up in felicitous recollections of a successful brick schoolhouse or jail." By the fall of 1872, while contractors continued to work on the house, the second floor was ready for occupancy and the Churches moved in. Additions and refinements to the interior, including all of the woodwork and the painted stenciling designed by Church, progressed virtually without a break into 1875; the last major internal component, the grand staircase, was completed in early 1876.

As initially constructed, Olana was inwardly spacious yet outwardly compact. The living areas were arranged around the central Court Hall on the ground floor. The largest room of that suite, the Dining Hall, at the northeast corner of the building (at right in pl. 10, and at far left in pl.11), which also served as a gallery to display the Churches' collection of Old Master paintings, rises a full two stories on the sloping site. The second story was divided between the Churches' bedrooms on the southeast and southwest, and the servants' quarters on the north and northwest, while the third floor was given over to the nursery on the northeast (marked by a two-column screen above the Dining Hall; pls. 9, 10) and to storage areas.

On the exterior, the principal visual accents were accorded to the upper floors, while boundaries between levels were deliberately blurred in favor of vertical cadence and coherence. The most prominent external feature, the tall tower on the southeast corner, comprises one of the living rooms (the East Parlor) on the ground floor, Mrs. Church's bedroom (with large balconied windows facing to the east and south; pls. 9, 13, 20, 21) on the floor above, and, beneath the roof, a capacious observation platform originally open on all four sides, where the family often had their tea and which also served as a sleeping porch on hot summer nights (pls. 22, 23). A narrow crow's nest, accessible via a steep wooden stair within the tower roof, opens at the very top (pl. 18). The painter's bedroom, from which many of the photographs in section II of this book were taken, is distinguished by an ornate oriel window projecting like a theater loge on the western facade. Restored in 1985 to the predominately dark color scheme it wore in 1888 (compare pls. 8, 9), the wooden window enframement resembles a piece of fine inlaid cabinetwork redefined for an architectural function.

The Persian character of Olana is both seriously and freely interpreted. Some of the ornamental details, in particular those that wreathe the interior arches spanning the Court hall, derive from *Monuments modernes de la Perse.* The conspicuous placement of those elements, plus the fact that the Churches collected furnishings from, books about and photographs of Persia into the 1890s, suggest that the couple regarded Olana as a model of Persian taste. A larger quantity of decorative ingredients on the exterior and interior are culled from *Les Arts Arabes,* which reproduces examples of Egyptian Islamic architecture and ornament. The east window of Mrs. Church's bedroom is an interesting case in point. Based on a plate in *Les Arts Arabes* of an entrance to a mosque in Alexandria, the design is noteworthy for twin pendants in front of the window tracery and for six-pointed stars — of which two appear in the Alexandrian prototype, versus three at Olana — in the lunette above (pl. 19). The stars probably induced the artist to select the motif, since in 1860 he had painted for his wife a small allegorical landscape, *The Star in the East* (still at Olana), to commemorate the first Christmas of their marriage. Other details, evidently, were composed without adherence to specific precedents. Church's drawings for the distinctive pattern of slates on the roof of the main tower (pl. 18) show that he experimented with several kaleidoscopic arrangements before settling on the one we see today.

During the dozen years after 1876, Church devised numerous improvements to the house. Most of them had to do with the interior decorative scheme, but from time to time the exterior received renewed attention: the window balconies on Mrs. Church's bedroom, for instance, were introduced as late as 1880. In June 1888, however, Church commenced a much larger undertaking — an addition on the southwest side that radically altered the physiognomy of the building. The extension, called the Studio Wing, was designed entirely by the artist and replaced a small, separate studio of about 1864, situated about halfway between the farm and the main house. Ironically, Church's capacity to make use of any such facility was by then greatly reduced. Increasing debilitation from rheumatism in the 1870s obliged him to curtail, then virtually to cease, painting; the last public exhibition of a recent Church picture took place in 1882. During the same period, he also gradually lost touch with new tastes

The Court Hall, Olana, 1884
New York State
Office of Parks, Recreation and Historic Preservation
Olana State Historic Site

18   THE SITTING ROOM, OLANA, 1988

in painting. Yet his curiosity about the world at large never faltered. Beginning in 1881, a sequence of wintertime journeys to Mexico to restore his health also generated fresh interests and revived older associations with the tropics. The earliest evidence within the fabric of Olana of that latest round of travels is a large cast-iron bell purchased in Mexico in 1886. It was installed the same year in the right-hand (north) arch on the east side of the main tower (see pls. 9, 22).

Composed of three basic elements — a colonnaded gallery, a combined studio and observation tower, and a semicircular porch on the northwest — the Studio Wing has attracted fewer compliments from twentieth-century commentators than the core of the building. While it is true that parts of the ensemble visually jostle one another and that structural defects — attributable to the precipitous site and to the fact that Church did not avail himself of a consulting architect for that phase of the building program — proved nettlesome from the outset, it is difficult to imagine the house without the extension. In conjunction with the gallery, the studio tower furnishes an effective counterweight to the southeast tower, the lacy colonnade (called the Piazza by the Churches) contrasts nicely with the heavier forms on the east, and the addition as a whole introduces a welcome horizontal accent to the design. The arches of the semicircular porch echo those of an earlier porch of rectangular shape on the original southwest corner of the building, so to that extent the Piazza and new porch represent an expansion and rearrangement of a previous feature. The immense bay window set in a wood enframement on the north wall (pl. 11) provides ample indirect light for a painter at his easel and complements the bay window of Church's bedroom on the opposite facade.

Stylistically, the Studio Wing dovetails with the earlier sections of the house as it signals the artist's many trips to Mexico. Each of the three thick corner pinnacles of the tower resembles an *almena*, a type of battlement recurrent in colonial Mexican churches, while the combination of flat roof, lengthy balustrade and the studio tower itself (pls. 14–16) recalls the *azeoteas* — open-air recreation spaces — that the Churches often encountered in Mexican hotels and townhouses.

Apart from stylistic considerations, the exterior of Olana in its completed form combines three underlying aspects. One of these, the ornamental polychromy from which the house obtains much of its Mediterranean character, also locates it within a wide spectrum of Victorian architecture. Buildings as diverse as Frank Furness' Pennsylvania Academy of the Fine Arts (1872–76) in Philadelphia, Calvert Vaux's and Frederick Withers' Jefferson Market Courthouse (1874–77; now the Jefferson Market Library) in New York City, and William Butterfield's Keble College (1868–82) in Oxford, England, are Olana's kin.

Another trait is the castellar solidity of Olana. Occasionally, the painter joked about his "feudal castle" and "bomb-proof edifice," but he and his wife would have found the sturdiness apposite in view of the exposed site on which the house stands, their knowledge that it literally rose from the soil (much of the stone came from the excavations, and from the quarry, pl. 138, near the present entrance to the estate), and their desire for privacy. Most important was both parents' wish to erect a dwelling that appeared able to protect their fragile family. Church's recommendation, written from Europe to a friend in 1869, to build with stone rather than with wood, and his boasts in the 1870s about the mass and thickness of Olana's lower walls, should be comprehended in terms of metaphoric as well as structural requirements for the house's stability.

The third characteristic, paradoxically, is the openness of the design. From the top of Sienghenbergh, the Churches and their guests could survey a panorama of breathtaking immensity, coherence, and beauty, looking down and across the Hudson River Valley toward the Catskill Mountains. The painter carefully adjusted the features of his home to take maximum advantage of those views. Especially on the south facade and also on the west and east, he positioned numbers of large windows, sizable unglazed openings and balconies, and multiple observation towers. Susan Hale (1833–1910), a capable artist and author and a sister of Edward Everett Hale, instantly recognized this quality during a visit in June 1884. "The house is large and all open on the lower floor, with wide doors and windows *à deux battants*, so that everywhere you look through vistas to shining oak boughs at hand, and dim, blue hills far beyond, middle distance omitted because so far below," she wrote. Her comments were seconded a few months later by Dr. Zabriskie, who observed that Olana was "a bright open eyed house, presenting on the landscape sides an almost unbroken expanse of plate-glass windows." In one instance, illusion was deemed more important than function. The central tower, which appears to be a four-sided gazebo, actually crowns the water circulation system of the building and is inaccessible from below. In the context of the entire composition, however, the water tower mediates effectively between its functional neighbors, enhancing the oriental flavor and highlighting the purpose of the building as a belvedere.

The process by which Church transformed Olana into a work of art in effect continues today. Thanks to the artist's youngest son Louis Church (1870–1943), and especially to Louis' wife, Sallie Good Church, who lived in the house until her death in 1964, Olana remains largely as its original owner left it in 1900. Alterations and deterioration that occurred during the second generation's occupancy are now being carefully mended by the New York State Office of Parks and Recreation and Historic Preservation, with the assistance of the Friends of Olana, a support organization founded in 1971 that has developed many projects to benefit the estate. Some of the photographs in this book (e.g. pl. 89) document these changes in-progress. After a few more seasons, the building will be returned, as far as possible, to its condition in 1891, when the Studio Wing was finished and Church delegated the management of the property to his son Louis. Visitors will then be able to enjoy even more fully the colorful exoticism, endless inventiveness, personal mementos and restorative variety that Olana offers.

Plate 1

Plate 3

PLATE 5

PLATE 6

PLATE 7

Plate 8

Plate 9 ▶

PLATE 10

PLATE II

PLATE 12

PLATE 13

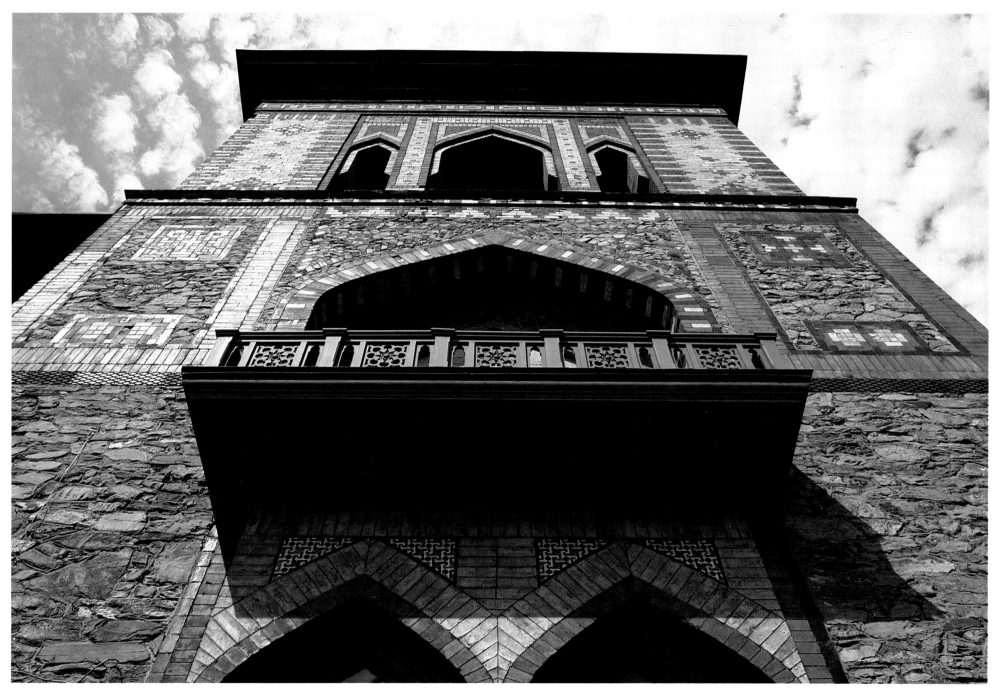

Plate 15

◀ Plate 14

PLATE 17

PLATE 16
(Left)

PLATE 18

PLATE 19

Plate 21

◀ Plate 20

Plate 23

Plate 22
(Left)

Plate 24
(Overleaf)

43

List of Plates

II

THE VIEW

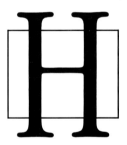is contemporaries agreed that Church had chosen an extraordinary location for his home. Early in 1867, several months before he purchased the summit of Sienghenbergh and three years before he began constructing Olana, a New York newspaper writer reported, "There are no finer views in the world than he can command from his windows." Nine years afterward, another commentator praised the site, declaring, "[It] commands so many views of varied character and beauty, that here may be almost said to culminate the glories of the Hudson. Here is the grandest and most impressive view of the Catskill Mountains." As a guest of the Churches mused in 1889, "The scene that spread before me filled me with regret that I had the soul of an artist without the power to wield the brush. It seemed the spot of all others to lend inspiration." Those authors sensed intuitively what the artist himself already knew full well: the scenic beauty of Olana would be as much a part of Church's legacy as his paintings.

Most visitors to Olana today will concur with those opinions. Olana is an inspiring, poetic place, and is so most of all because of the views arrayed from the top of the hill. Hundreds of exquisitely arranged square miles of the earth's surface are spread invitingly at one's feet. The horizon to the south and west appears to curve, suggesting the sphere of the earth itself. The seasons proclaim their passing in pageants of fecundity and color that seem more resplendent here than elsewhere in the region. Weather systems track across the landscape, at times level with and even below one's vantage point. Arresting cloud formations gather over the distant mountains and drift across the valley. Lanced with sunbeams during the day, stained with roseate hues at sunrise or sunset, enlivened by prismatic tints of an evanescent rainbow, the clouds lend varying degrees of energy, repose, or solemnity, as well as diversity and scale to the scenery. On the clearest days, as nineteenth-century witnesses were fond of pointing out, one can see nearly sixty miles south to West Point and more than thirty-five miles north past Albany. At other times, visibility may be reduced to just a few yards.

The geographic environment of Olana is the stage upon which the daily dramas of atmosphere and illumination take place. The foremost ingredient is the Hudson River, which defines the entire valley. To the west, the ridge of Sienghenbergh drops off abruptly, offering glimpses of the river through screens of woodland that have thickened considerably since Church's day. Roger's Island and the Rip Van Winkle Bridge, erected in 1935 and partly resting on the island, are the major objects here. To the southwest and south, by contrast, the terrain descends gently along avenues of trees, directing the eye toward the river, which reappears three miles away in a broad basin called the Bend in the River. All geographic elements in the Olana panorama pivot on the shimmering, often strongly reflective surface of this stretch of the waterway. On the Churches' own property, the lake (see Section IV) complements the distant river basin. Toward the southeast and east, trees again shield prospects the Churches enjoyed, though here and there an opening discloses nearby features, notably Blue Hill (see pl. 33), two miles away. Vistas originally open to Mount Merino (see pls. 1, 32), a hill of elongated proportions, larger than Sienghenbergh and just to the north of it, are now almost completely obscured by trees.

West of the Hudson River and running parallel to it is the eastern range of the Catskill Mountains. It was beneath and occasionally among these slopes that Church received from Thomas Cole the training that served him for the rest of his life. As a mature artist, Church could not have contrived for one of his paintings a highland backdrop of more elegant configurations than the Catskills as seen from Olana. The progression begins about twenty miles to the southwest with four mountains — Overlook, Plattekill, Indian Head and Twin — which together make up the Sleeping Giant or Old Man in the Mountain. The next summits of note, Kaaterskill High Peak and Kaaterskill Round Top, stand as central objects in many of Cole's paintings. These are followed by South Mountain and North Mountain, projecting like a pair of broad shoulders some twelve miles away, and Stopple Point, which looms behind them farther to the north. After falling at Dutchner's Notch north of Stopple Point, the escarpment quickly rises again to form Blackhead Mountain, then gradually descends past Windham High Peak on the northwest. The distance from one end of the chain to the other is approximately thirty-five miles. Open horizon beckons on the northwest, but additional eminences are visible to the south.

Although the far-off topography on the east is not as distinguished as that on the west, the Taconic and the Berkshire mountains extend low profiles for dozens of miles against the sunrise. The pyramidal shape of Greylock Mountain, the most emphatic in the combined ranges seen from Olana, projects about fifteen miles away to the east southeast.

Throughout his life, Church was instinctively attuned to all manner of "fine things hung in the sky," to use a phrase he wrote from Olana in 1870. Cloud formations could suggest animals, human beings, or parts and combinations thereof; a star might assume the shape of the Cross, and the moon take on the guise of a mythological charioteer — that is, Church occasionally interspersed these and other flights of fancy with his realistic portrayals of natural phenomena. Seemingly unpaintable meteorlogical events, such as rainbows and aurora borealis, sharpened his powers of perception and challenged his technical and interpretive faculties in major canvases. Twilight and, to a lesser extent, sunrise, when the firmament blankets the earth with color, were his favorite times of day. He shared that preference with countless contemporaries in all walks of life, among them Baron Alexander von Humboldt (1769–1859), the great Prussian geographer whose writings inspired Church to travel in South America in 1853 and 1857. Yet the love of early evening skies, and the mixture of spiritual reflection, reverence, exultation and mournfulness they aroused in nineteenth-century beholders, were perhaps stronger in Church than in any other member of his generation. Olana provided the ideal setting in which he could perpetuate and gratify those emotions, and witness the entire repertoire of nature's celestial displays.

Comments in his correspondence and dozens of sketches in oil and pencil executed between 1860 and the mid-1890s attest to Church's abiding attachment to the landscape that enveloped his estate. From several vantage points on the property (most frequently, from his old studio, between the farm and the main house), he recorded sunsets of every shape and intensity, as well as shifting seasons and weather patterns, passing thunderstorms, fogbanks, phases of the moon, aurora borealis, comets and occasional brilliant meteors. The majority of his oil studies of views looking southeast, south and west, a small selection of which is reproduced in these pages, were painted during the early 1870s, when Church was closely involved in the construction of Olana. He had approximately ten of these works, one of his own larger oil paintings, and two small oils of the same subjects by a colleague, Arthur Parton (1842–1914), framed to adorn the interiors of Olana by the early 1890s.

The Church family and their guests were as irresistibly attracted to the spectacles outside Olana's windows as was the artist himself. Grace King (1851–1932), a writer from New Orleans, encapsulated visitors' experiences for her own and following generations in June 1887. After accepting an invitation from Mrs. Church to observe a sunset from the bell tower, she wrote to a friend: "I am not going to describe the sunset to you, but I felt all through it that we ought to be looking at it on our knees."

PLATE 25 ▶

Plate 27

◄ Plate 26

PLATE 28

PLATE 29

PLATE 30
PLATE 31
(Overleaves)

PLATE 32

PLATE 33 ▶

PLATE 34

PLATE 35 ▶

PLATE 36

PLATE 37

PLATE 38

PLATE 39

Plate 40

Plate 41 ▶

Plate 42

PLATE 43

PLATE 44

PLATE 45

Plate 46

PLATE 47

Plate 48

Plate 49
(Right)

Plate 50
(Far Right)

PLATE 51

Plate 52

Plates 53–58
(Overleaves)

PLATE 59

PLATE 60

PLATE 61

PLATE 62

PLATE 63

PLATE 64 ▶

PLATE 66

◀ PLATE 65

PLATE 67

PLATE 68 ▶

PLATE 69

II

List of Plates

III

THE PARK

Every attentive visitor to Olana should inspect the farm on which Church and his family resided between 1861 and 1872. Situated approximately five hundred yards southeast of the main house, the farm now consists of seven buildings positioned within a short distance of one another: the white clapboard cottage (today covered with white shingles) originally designed by Richard Morris Hunt in 1860, two red barns, a shed and a pump house also painted red, a white board-and-batten utility shed north of the cottage, and, nestled next to a flourishing apple orchard, a ruined eighteenth-century farmhouse erected by Winsum Brisee. The concrete foundations of an ample edifice, probably a pig house, remain in the pasture one hundred yards farther to the south, and the outlines of two other constructions can be discerned near the southeast corner of the lake. These buildings and remnants were complemented during the Churches' lifetimes by up to fifteen additional structures, including the artist's original studio, which have since disappeared.

The larger of the two barns, called the Main Barn, is an impressive sight from almost any perspective. Straddling a sloping site in an L-shaped plan, it comprises a massive dairy wing built in 1899 on the east, abutted on the northwest by a hay barn built in 1867, and a trio of storage sheds erected in 1886 on the west. Within the dairy block, there are four interior stories. A cement-and-stone retaining wall, probably designed to prevent grazing animals from falling over a shale precipice (pl. 136), extends from the southwest corner of the dairy block. The wall is also a late addition, replacing a split-rail fence that must have served the same purpose. The smaller barn (1860–61), known as the Farm Stable, sheltered farm horses and their feed. In the late nineteenth century this sizable structure was augmented by capacious wings on the south and the west. The animals that pulled the donkey cart, three carriages and three sleds (a fraction of the vehicles once owned by the Churches) preserved in the carriage house (1870) at the top of the hill, were quartered in the carriage house itself. The small shed immediately east of the Farm Stable and the engine house on the other side of the dirt farm road date from about 1870 and 1886, respectively.

Cozy Cottage, as the Churches affectionately called their first home on the property, began life as a modest L-shaped building, which the painter quickly reconfigured to a T by adding a kitchen at the northeast end. Immediately following his return from Europe and the Near East, he introduced a large bedroom wing on the west side. Besides providing increased accommodation for his burgeoning family during that busy period, the second extension served as a preliminary exercise for his work on the new house. An unfinished oil study (still at Olana) by the artist, presumably painted during the early 1870s before the main house was occupied, portrays this sprawling yet quaint four-segment structure, its lower walls garlanded with colorful vines. On the whole, the couple led an idyllic life on the farm during the 1860s, and their last two children were born there as the new domicile was under construction. As his wife sat "under the apple trees in luxurious contemplation of the beautiful scenes which encircle our cottage" in May 1870, Church commemorated the superabundant apple blossoms of that season and, one might surmise, the rich familial associations of the farm in general, in a small painting now hanging in the East Parlor of Olana. After the Churches moved to the top of the hill, the cottage was maintained as a guest lodging and, later on, as residence for farm workers, while the farm continued to fulfill its agrarian functions. The cottage endured a roughhanded reduction to its original size in the 1950s and remains unused today.

The landscape setting of Olana is composed of two basic parts. The smaller one consists of the lawns and terraces near the main house. These provide a pedestal and cloth of honor for the building and carpets of manicured greenery on which family members and guests could congregate near the main entrance and take in the view to the southwest. The flower garden below the stone terrace on the southeast was installed in the late 1880s. The conspicuous High Victorian gardenesque planting on the carriage turnaround northeast of the house made its first appearance during the tenure of Louis and Sallie Church. Assembled from two green annuals (elephant ears and castor beans) and two red ones (salvia and canna), it attains an architectonic stature at full growth during late August and September (pl. 94).

The larger part is the park itself, which always has been left wild, but is the product of thoughtful planning by Church over a thirty-year period. The appearance of the park between the farm, the lake and the main house is now somewhat changed from Church's time. Aside from the increased overall height of wooded areas on the property, the greatest differences are in the numbers of trees south of Olana and their positioning. Throughout the grassy clearing that now stretches almost unbroken to the northern shore of the lake, individual trees and groups of trees were distributed to diversify and rechannel vistas in both directions, particularly those prospects leading toward the house from below, without closing them off entirely. The effect can be partially re-created today by walking among the trees on the slope southeast of the house.

These and other subtly cultivated features of the grounds were shaped according to the aesthetic principles of the Sublime, Beautiful and Picturesque, formulated in England during the eighteenth century and widely influential on European and American architecture, painting and sculpture as well as landscape gardening by the middle of the nineteenth century. The house itself partakes of a Picturesque, multifaceted composition, so that no view of it is exactly like any other and none predicts any other, and of a Sublime monumentality, especially in the southeast tower. The landscape setting retains the outlines of a similar aesthetic organization, but its Picturesque qualities previously were amplified by the sequence and studied naturalness of glimpses of the house offered to spectators ascending the hill via the original carriage road. These now-you-see-it, now-you-don't foretastes would have excited visitors' expectations and absorbed their attention until their goal, the building itself, was reached. Only at the turn of the road east of the main entrance did the trees part to reveal an unobstructed prospect of Olana across the lawn (pl. 10). A few steps away in front of the south facade, guests would have turned to find — as they do today — the Sublime expanse of the Hudson Valley suddenly revealed.

Church directed those aspects of Olana as he did all others. From 1860 onward and especially in 1867, when his acquisition of the summit of

Sienghenbergh was assured, he carefully planted acres of deciduous trees —
oaks,maples, elms, birches, chestnuts and others — and various evergreens.
These were joined by large numbers of additional trees in the late 1880s, a
period of revived landscaping activity. The birches (descendants of those
introduced by the artist) are the most effective botanical gestures near the
house (see pls. 5, 81, 82), although also the least stable, because their root
systems cannot obtain a good grip in the rocky soil.

It is known that Mrs. Church was an avid gardener, that she and her husband
were enchanted by flowering fruit trees on the farm, and that she and her
daughter enjoyed picking wildflowers in the park, but the profusion of
wildflowers that now adorns the grounds from May through late fall seems to
be a twentieth-century phenomenon. The seasonal sequence begins with
dogwood, followed by dame's rocket, daisies, clover, coreopsis, black-eyed
Susans, wild aster, day lilies, loosetrife, Queen Anne's lace and goldenrod,
among others; flowers of the last-named species can persist until November.
The outpouring of natural "bloom" — to use Church's favorite nomenclature —
is augmented by domesticated species such as apple, lilac, forsythia, wisteria,
trumpet vines, bottlebrush and wild barberries. The coreopsis has been
remarkably luxuriant in recent years. Mingled with white daisies, tall white
grass, red clover, purple asters, and up to a dozen additional flowering plants, its
yellow blossoms blanket the fields in mid-June with an outpouring of color
rivaling that of the most intense fall foliage.

PLATE 70 ▶

PLATE 71

PLATE 72

PLATE 73

PLATE 74

PLATE 75

PLATE 76

PLATE 77

PLATE 78
(Right)

PLATE 79

PLATE 80

Plate 82

◄ Plate 81

PLATE 83

PLATE 84

Plate 85

PLATE 86

Plate 88

PLATE 89

PLATE 90
(Right)

Plate 92

◄ Plate 91

PLATE 93

PLATE 94

PLATE 95
(Overleaf)

III
List of Plates

IV

THE LAKE

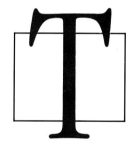he lake is the largest feature on the Olana estate. It is not a natural formation, yet neither is it entirely an artificial one. When Church purchased his first piece of property here in 1860, he found, where the lake now stands, a neglected swamp in which two pools were fed by an indeterminant number (seven, by a recent estimate) of gurgling springs. Exactly when he hit upon the idea of converting that waste acreage into a visual keynote is not known for certain, but it is likely that in pondering the problem, he decided on some aspects of the solution seen today almost immediately. In a treatise published in 1853 titled *Landscape Gardening: Or, Parks and Pleasure Grounds,* a copy of which is still in Church's library, Charles H. J. Smith declared, "Of the varied material in the composition of natural scenery, there is none that produces more beauty, variety and interest than water." The size and shape of the lake at Olana, as well as the fact that it was not fully established before 1873, suggest that the final formulation was contemporaneous with the new house.

To construct the lake, the artist engaged farm laborers to remove tons of peat (which with characteristic frugality he had recycled on his crop fields, sold to neighboring farmers, and may have used to reshape portions of the park), to dam up the resultant water accumulation, and to channel the overspill into an existing small creek at the southeast corner of the new basin. After meandering past neighboring land now occupied by Columbia-Greene Community College, the stream joins with other freshets on the opposite side of Route 23, past the former home of Church's physician, Dr. Gustavus A. Sabine, and flows into the Hudson River.

The lake covers about eight acres, more or less in the shape of an elongated right-hand mitten seen palm up. Viewed in a foreshortened perspective from the top of Sienghenbergh, however, it closely approximates a mirror image of the Bend in the River, the lakelike widening of the Hudson River some three miles south of Olana. To effect this binary relationship, the painter must have carefully calculated in advance the contours of his reservoir as they would be perceived from the new house. The lake is therefore essentially a scenic device, integral with both the building from which it was meant to be observed and the larger surrounding environment. From the intended vantage point, it becomes a source of light — a looking glass capturing a fragment of sky within the boundaries of the Churches' landholding — and an extension of that landholding into the entire river valley.

In addition to its role as a distant focal point of visual attention, the lake furnished a foreground (or, more precisely, a forewater) to magnify the prospects across it, and provided a recreation space for the family and a resource for the farm. In the early 1880s, Church constructed an ornamental road around the perimeter of the lake so that his family and guests could avail themselves of the new scenic possibilities. Whether or not he sketched on that avenue is difficult to say (one oil study of a lakeside carriageway, now in the Cooper-Hewitt Museum in New York, *may* have been painted at Olana), but the careful planning of the road itself, plus the evidence of numerous late nineteenth-century photographs still at Olana taken by Louis Church, which show the house perched above the water and general views of the lake, demonstrate the father's, as well as the son's, sensitivities. Some of the photos illustrate rowboats tethered along the shore, and flocks of tame ducks and geese in the water. In warm weather the lake served as a reservoir for the farm, and in winter it produced ice for use all year round.

The principal views of Olana from across the lake are obtained at a spot that the Churches called Picnic Point, located in the curve between the mitten's thumb and forefinger; on the road above the southern tip of the lake; and through vistas deliberately opened on the road above the eastern shore (pls. 121, 122). A modern path along the southeast shore provides two or three additional fine vantage points, although for most of its length the house is concealed by trees. From those positions, the scenic menu is rich indeed. Dissipating fog at dawn produces spectacular unveilings of the distant house and the nearer shoreline foliage. A summer sunrise under calm conditions and a blustery early autumn morning can be equally breathtaking (pls. 103, 104). Afternoon sunlight often

defines the same scenes with the sharpness of a daguerreotype, yet at that hour, too, varied atmospheres can induce a wide spectrum of colors, lighting, reflectance and evocative cloud forms.

By itself, the lake presents many interesting tableaux. Perhaps the choicest can be found around the curvature of its eastern end, near the farm. On misty mornings, the trees bordering the shore are suspended in perfect reflections (pl. 114), and the forested hillock just south of the crescent seems to float free of its land moorings and become a wedge-shaped island (pls. 98, 113).

Today, the lake plays host to an assortment of animal and plant life. Most of the fauna, including small fish, large tortoises, myriad frogs (pl. 131) and occasional transient waterbirds, are exceedingly shy, so visitors should not expect to have their experience measurably enhanced by them. In winter, when the water surface freezes sufficiently and while the snow cover remains thin, two other local lake-users make an appearance — the figure skater and the hockey player. These amateur athletes (who must always check with Olana State Historic Site staff before venturing onto the ice) follow in the skate marks of the Church children, who could turn pretty figures while their parents, then infirm, sat on the sidelines or sought warmer climes elsewhere.

PLATE 96 ▶

PLATE 97

PLATE 98

PLATE 100

PLATE 99
(Left)

PLATE 101

PLATE 102

PLATE 103

PLATE 104

Plate 106

Plate 108

◀ Plate 107

Plate 109

Plate 110
(Right)

PLATE III

PLATE 112

Plate 114

PLATE 115

PLATE 116

PLATE 117
(Overleaf)

IV
List of Plates

V

ROADS, WOODS, SEASONS

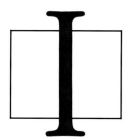f the view from Olana can be called an immense canvas upon which nature, with Church's assistance, composes images of infinite permutations, the park below potentially represents a studio full of smaller canvases over which the artist could exercise his own considerable control.

He did exactly that. His transformation of unused wetland into a lake and his introduction of thousands of trees throughout the estate already have been described. By the time the Studio Wing was nearing completion in September 1890, the *Boston Herald* reporter noted in his article, "An artificial lake several acres in extent adds to the diversity of the scene, and the multitude of trees planted by Mr. Church a quarter century ago give evidence of the wise foresight and prompt action when he came here. It may not be inappropriately said: 'A wood coeval with himself he sees,/ And loves his own contemporary trees.' "

To mold his domain, as well as to render it accessible, Church became a road builder. Soon after he arrived at Olana in 1860, he began expanding the existing network of farm roads and developing a system of approach routes and scenic carriageways. That first phase of road engineering occupied him on and off for much of the decade and again in 1869–70, during the initial construction period of the new house. A second phase of intense activity spanned the early and mid-1880s. A few further adjustments were made under Louis Church in the early twentieth century, and the present paved arteries were laid during the late 1960s, after Olana had become a public preserve.

Three approach avenues, each of a different character, were designed by Church: the South Road (pl. 123), now adapted for motor vehicles leaving the site; the Bethune Road, named for the previous owner of a parcel of land on the escarpment southwest of the house; and the North Road, to the north and east of the house. The last two are maintained as spacious footpaths through the woods, as are a long section of the Lake Road and the lengths of two other carriage drives: the Ridge Road, linking the Bethune and North roads, which offers dramatic glimpses of Olana from below (pl. 4) and an overlook across the Hudson River; and Crown Hill Road, a meandering cul-de-sac fastened to the eastern arm of the Lake Road, which is oriented to distant and now largely concealed views of the house and the farm from the summit of Crown Hill. A dirt road winding through the frontage park a short distance south of the house, introduced by the artist around 1887, was his final effort in thoroughfare design. The paved road currently used by motor vehicles entering the site (pl. 124) comprises segments of a farm road adjacent to the Quarry, the western arm of the Lake Road, and a modern spur west of the farm near the track of an earlier farm road.

The original shale-gravel surfaces of the nineteenth-century thoroughfares, their tree-lined edges and of course their careful planning, visually differentiated them from their natural surroundings as well as from farm roads on the property. Functionally they were distinct, too, since carriage travel in warm weather and sleigh rides in winter became favorite pastimes at Olana. Nimble visitors, such as Susan Hale, also went for long walks for the sheer pleasure of it, though in 1884 she had to confess weariness at the inevitable reascent: "In that just so much as you go down you have to climb up again, being on the very top of everything." Along the eastern arm of the Lake Road, the Churches and their friends delighted in a deliberately contrived vista of the house emerging through a frame of trees (pls. 121, 122). And at every turn they were treated to touchable natural details analogous to those in the foregrounds of Church's paintings.

The park was and remains a naturalist-outdoorsman-artist's laboratory. Patches of the forest, for example, resemble some of Church's oil studies from the late 1870s of dense Maine woodlands, and may have partly inspired his small *Jungle Interior* composition painted in 1891 and now hanging in the Studio at Olana. Today's hikers will discover individual specimens of autumn foliage that

are as vibrant as any ensemble seen from a distance. Landscape and buildings alike are especially picturesque just after a winter snowfall. Forests that in summer appear impenetrable are laid bare; woods, trails, and meadows merge imperceptibly with one another; the lake becomes a huge white surface modulated only by shadows, and cracks and reflections in melting ice; and the most irregular natural and man-made forms acquire a pristine freshness. It is as if those who follow in the Churches' sled tracks a century later are the first to confront these scenes.

The frail health of both Church and Mrs. Church prevented them from spending many winters at Olana after the road system was complete. Yet the painter's decreasing ability to work at his easel toward the end of his life also spurred him to greater exertions at Olana itself. Extensive tree plantings, the finest scenic roads and the Studio Wing all date from that period. In 1884, amidst a fervor of road building, Church wrote to a friend about making "more and better landscapes in this way than by tampering with paint and canvas in the studio." The remark is indicative not so much of vexation with old age, but rather of the quarter-century of effort he had already invested in Olana, and of his continuing creative urges, undiminished self-confidence and abiding love for the out-of-doors in general and the Catskill Mountain region of the Hudson Valley in particular. On the three-dimensional canvas that is Olana, he created a major monument of nineteenth-century American culture, one comparable to the entirety of his life's work as a studio artist. Olana became Frederic Church's last great preoccupation, and his last great work of art.

PLATE 118 ▶

Plate 120

◄ Plate 119

PLATE 122

PLATE 121
(Left)

PLATE 123

PLATE 124

PLATE 128

PLATE 129

PLATE 130

PLATE 131
(Right)

164

Plate 133

◄ Plate 132

167

Plate 135

◀ Plate 134

PLATE 136

PLATE 137 ▶

PLATE 138

PLATE 139

Plate 141

◀ Plate 140

PLATE 142

PLATE 143 ▶

PLATE 144
(Overleaf)

List of Plates

Technical Note

All of the photographs in this book were taken on Kodachrome 64 film. Nikon equipment was employed throughout, Nikkor lenses serving for the following plates: *20mm F2.8:* 16, 21, 22, 26, 36, 37, 50, 73, 98, 109, 111, 120, 124, 136, 137, 138, 140, 141; *28mm PC F3.5:* 2, 6, 7, 8, 9, 10, 11, 12, 13, 14, 15, 23, 24, 28, 30, 31, 32, 33, 34, 35, 46, 47, 59, 61, 62, 66, 67, 68, 71, 72, 74, 76, 79, 80, 81, 82, 86, 87, 88, 94, 103, 104, 105, 113, 115, 119, 123, 125, 134; *35mm PC F2.8:* 25, 48, 49, 51, 52, 60, 63, 64, 65, 69, 89, 90, 91, 112, 118, 132, 144; *50mm F2:* 1, 2, 70, 97; *55mm F3.5:* 27, 29, 83, 84, 102, 108, 126, 130, 131, 133, 135; *75–150mm F3.5:* 4, 5, 38, 39, 45, 53, 54, 55, 56, 57, 58, 77, 78, 85, 92, 93, 95, 96, 106, 107, 110, 114, 116, 121, 123, 127, 128, 129, 139, 142, 143; *105mm F2.5:* 103; *200mm F4:* 17, 19, 20, 40, 41, 42, 43, 44, 75, 99, 100, 117; *300mm F4.5:* 3, 18.

Writings About Olana

The following list is divided into two parts, the first consisting of the most important articles and books published during the Churches' lifetimes which refer to Olana, and the second of modern publications, theses and reports in which Olana is an essential subject. Both portions of the list are arranged chronologically.

I

"The Kaatskills. Their Attractions Enthusiastically Set Forth. Prospects of the Present Season. Artists Among the Mountains." Clipping from an unidentified (New York?) journal, ca. 1871–72, in Bronck Museum, Coxsackie, New York.

"Residence of Mr. Church, the Artist." *New York Art Journal* 2 (June 1876), pp. 247–48.

French, H.W. "Frederick Edwin Church," in French *Art and Artists in Connecticut* (Boston and New York: Lee and Shepard; Charles Dillingham, 1878), pp. 130–31.

"An Aesthetic Frolic." *New York World,* 24 May 1879, p. 5.

Zabriskie, Francis Nicholl. " 'Old Colony Papers.' An Artist's Castle, and our Ride thereto." *New York Christian Intelligencer,* 10 September 1884, p. 2.

"The American Rhine." *New York World,* 21 July 1889, p. 11.

Bonnelle, Frank J. "In Summer Time at Olana." *Boston Sunday Herald,* 7 September 1890, p. 17.

II

Scully, Vincent. "Palace of the Past." *Progressive Architecture* 46 (May 1965), pp. 184–89.

Huntington, David C. "Olana — 'the Center of the World.' " *Antiques* 88 (November 1965), pp. 656–63.

_____. *The Landscapes of Frederic Edwin Church* (New York: George Braziller, 1966), pp. 114–25.

"An Imperiled American Treasure." *Life* 60 (13 May 1966), pp. 64–80.

Goss, Peter. "An Investigation of Olana, the Home of Frederic Edwin Church, Painter." Ph.D Dissertation, Ohio University, Athens, Ohio, 1973.

Kerr, Joan Paterson. "Olana." *American Heritage* 26 (August 1975), pp. 38–44.

Goss, Peter. "Olana — the Artist as Architect." *The Magazine Antiques* 110 (October 1976), pp. 764–75.

O'Sullivan, Thomas. "The Studio Wing of Olana." M.A. Thesis, State University of New York College at Oneonta at its Cooperstown Graduate Programs, 1980.

Aslet, Clive. "Olana, New York State." *Country Life* 124 (22 September 1983), pp. 761–65; (29 September 1983), pp. 839–42.

Ryan, James A. "The Master Plan for Olana State Historic Site." M.A. Thesis, State University of New York College at Oneonta at its Cooperstown Graduate Programs, 1984.

Toole, R.M. "Historic Landscape Report for Olana State Historic Site, Hudson, New York 12534." Prepared for the New York State Office of Parks, Recreation and Historic Preservation, 31 July 1984.

Zukowsky, John, and Stimson, Robbe Pierce, *Hudson River Villas* (New York: Rizzoli, 1985), pp. 200–205.

Lesser, Ellen McClelland. "Landscape Research Report for Olana State Historic Site, Hudson, New York 12534." Prepared for the New York State Office of Parks, Recreation and Historic Preservation, 15 August 1986.

Stein, Roger B. "Artifact as Ideology: The Aesthetic Movement in its American Context," in *In Pursuit of Beauty: Americans and the Aesthetic Movement* (New York: Metropolitan Museum of Art / Rizzoli, 1986), pp. 23–51.

Carr, Gerald L. "Frederic Edwin Church as a Public Figure," in Franklin Kelly and Gerald L. Carr, *The Early Landscapes of Frederic Edwin Church, 1845–1854* (Fort Worth: Amon Carter Museum, 1987), pp. 1–30.

Rhoads, William B. "The Artist's House and Studio in the Nineteenth-Century Hudson Valley and Catskills," in Sandra Philips and Linda Weintraub, eds., *Charmed Places: Hudson River Artists and Their Houses, Studios, and Vistas* (New York: Bard College and Harry N. Abrams, 1988), pp. 77–97.

Huntington, David C. "Olana — the Center of the Center of the World," in Irving Lavin, ed., *World Art: Themes of Unity and Diversity, XXVIth International Congress of the History of Art* (University Park: Pennsylvania State University Press, 1989), pp. 767–774.

Ryan, James A. "Frederic Church's Olana: Architecture and Landscape as Art," in Franklin Kelly et al., *Frederic Edwin Church* (Washington, D.C.: National Gallery of Art, 1989; forthcoming).